Healing

For your brokenness

By

Dianne King-Walker

Copyright ©2022 Dianne King Walker

All rights reserved. No part of this publication may be reproduced, distributed, or transmitted in any form or by any means, including photocopying, recording, or other electronic or mechanical methods, without the prior written permission of the publisher, except in the case of brief quotations embodied in critical reviews and certain other noncommercial uses permitted by copyright law.

ISBN: 978-1-951300-38-8

Liberation's Publishing – West Point - Mississippi

Dedication

This book is dedicated to the memory of my brother, Pastor Jessie King Sr whose courageous preaching of the gospel, great love for God, and godly lifestyle, inspired me to seek a closer relationship to God.

Table of Content

Introduction 7

Chapter 1: The Man 9

    Jesus Will Supply Our Needs 19

    Testimony 21

    Jesus Waits Long for Us 25

    Testimony 30

    Jesus Is an On Time God 33

Chapter Two: The Woman 37

    The Need of a Personal Relationship 37

    Testimony 42

Chapter Three: The Message 49

    Testimony 54

    The Ministry 55

    Healing 59

    Health 66

    Wholeness 70

Note from the Author 75

Prayer for Healing 77

From Brokenness to Wholeness

Epilogue 79

Introduction

Life can be what we make it, happy, and wonderful with God on our side. The Man literally takes my breath away! He came that his people could have life, and yet many people are stuck in the pain of their past and haven't been able to move past all the hurt to find the healing they need. The scars of sin are deep and lasting, but of pain and hurt that people go through, only God can heal. He can supply all of His people's needs. There is nothing that's too hard for God. Even though you may feel as if there is no help for your situation, God, is able.

God is long suffering. He waits a long time on his children because he is love, and he loves them just that much. And only he knows how much time his people need. He is never late; he is always on time. Whenever he gets there it's on time. We might think he is late, but he never is. He is such a loving and caring God that doesn't mind going out of his way for you. It's good to know him, and just good to know, he knows you. It's an awesome thing to have a good relationship with such a good God. He has placed eternity in all his people's heart, so that we are not satisfied without him everything we need is in him.

God draws us in and blesses us with his Holy Spirit which leads us through life. In his loving care he gives us a reason for living. He guides us through the dark terrains of life. He heals us and makes us whole. Then, he gives us purpose to help and lead others to salvation.

After a lifetime of hurt and brokenness, to finally have peace about the hurts of the past, to be made whole in your body, mind, and soul. God allows us to endure trails and tragedies, but he don't want his people to stay stuck, focusing on the hurts and pain but focus on the result that the pain will bring come. It's the pain and hard times that have made us who we are in Christ and helped us to make the decision to sell out for God and be the people we are in Christ.

It's due to him, never forget he is an all-knowing God and knows what best for all his children. There is a reason God allows things to happen to us in our life. It's those things that made us strong solders for him.

This is a story of a woman's journey to healing, health, and wholeness. This is also my journey, and I know it may be many of yours out there as well. This is why God led me through writing this book, so that others maybe helped as I was. God can fill your very being. He can make you whole. To God be the glory for all he has done! And going to do.

Chapter 1: The Man

I am excited. I am sitting at my desk with thoughts swirling around in my mind of a savior that gave so much. He did so much and is still doing so much for the people he created. I am one of those people, it is hard to contain my joy. As I begin this chapter on "the man," it is imperative that I attempt to introduce this man to you. This is no ordinary man. This man was one hundred percent man and at the same time one hundred percent God. This man pulled off his divinity and robed himself in flesh, left his home in glory, came to earth for a span of time, to secure his people safely and lovingly. His people needed a savior to pay their sin debt. He was the only one worthy and able to redeem mankind.

God so love the world he gave his only begotten son, and that same Son gave his life so his people could live. His people, his creation, humans, male and female, had fallen from grace and lost their spiritual connection with God. So, God had already set the plan in place to reconcile his people back to himself. This man who came from the father was conceived of the Holy Ghost, through a virgin name Mary. As a child he grew in knowledge and wisdom. At the age of twelve he was in the synagogue learning and teaching. His first miracle was at a wedding in a place called Canna of Galilee where he turned water into wine. He healed the sick, made the lame to walk, gave sight to the blind, caused the dumb to speak, and raised the dead. He holds this entire world in his hands.

This man is (Omnipresent) everywhere at the same time. He is (Omniscient) he knows everything meaning nothing is hidden from him. He is (Omnipotent) he has all power, he can handle any situation or problem, and he is (Immutable) he never changes. His love for us will never change. This man is perfect, and perfection cannot be improved upon. He is Alpha and Omega the beginning and the end. He is the King of Kings and the Lord of Lords. He is our sacrificial lamb, the rose of Sharon, the lily of the valley, and the bright and morning star. He is, I am, whatever we need him to be, he can be.

After this lengthy introduction, it still pales in the sight of who he really is. Try as we may, the words have not been invented that could accurately describe him. Who is he to me? He is my everything. To name a few more things, he is my reason for being. Life makes no sense without him my Lord, my savior, my peace, my joy, my light in darkness, my God, my all, and all. He is my hiding place. the one I run to when things get bad and overwhelming. And this only skims the surface of what he has been and is to me.

And when I say he is my everything I mean my world centers around him. When I wake up in the morning my thoughts are of him. I immediately start thanking him. I then seek him on the things I must do, and how he wants me to go about doing them. The plans I have is of how to glorify him, and how to make him happy in all I do in my life. I want to please him. Now mind you I don't always follow through. I sometimes fall short, but I always fall forward trying to do his will. When I lay down at night, he is my last thought. I'm thanking him for my day and asking for his protection through the night.

That's what I mean when I say he is my everything. In all I do I try to make him my priority. I also said he is my reason for being. Not only is he, our creator. He is also our only redeemer and savior. He created us, and he gave his life as a ransom for us when we messed up. Without him and his redemptive plan there would be no me or you. This is why I say he is my reason for being. My life makes no sense without him because he is my hiding place. When the world gets mean and cold, I can run to him. When I say he makes everything alright, he makes everything alright. I know why I am, and who I am, and what I am.

I know what I should be doing and when I don't know, he does. And when I put my trust in him it all makes sense. He is my Lord. He rules my life I look to him for whatever I need. I live my life according to his guidelines so that makes him my Lord and savior. As I said earlier, he saved me redeemed me and set me free from the bondage of sin. Now I live in the freedom of God. He gives me peace in the mist of my storms and troubles. No matter what is going on in my life I can always find peace in him. His peace surpasses all understanding. People wonder why I am not flipping out. How am I holding it together? They can't understand his peace because his peace is not as the world's peace, temporary. God's peace lasts a lifetime. He is also my joy.

The joy of the Lord is our strength. This joy keeps you holding on when things get bad in your life. This is why you don't take your own life as some do, but you hang in there until things turn around. This joy no one can take away because it's from the inside. It doesn't come from anything that's happening on the outside. This is due to the fact that he is always with you on the inside of you. That in itself is enough to shout about all by itself. He is my light in dark times. Oh my God!

I don't know if you have ever had any dark times, but I have had some really dark times that I thought would break me. But my God Always brought me through, always. I am not sad about my dark days. When I look back over my life, it was my dark days that I found God the closest to me. As I write this book right now, I am experiencing some of those dark days, my heart is heavy, but I know God has me, holding me, and keeping me, carrying me through and comforting me. He is a very present help in times of need.

Whatever comes in my life, I know without a shadow of doubt that it's not too hard for God. I have been through a lot. When I see others and some of the situation that they are in or going through it makes me realize how blessed I am. I see just how merciful God has been to me. He doesn't give me what I deserve. In case you think you don't deserve whatever you may be going through at this time, the wage of sin is death. Everyone is going through something at some time in their life. But God so loved the world that he took our punishment upon himself and let all that will accept him as Lord, live.

He said of himself that he was the Rose of Sharon. Of all the flowers that God has made, the rose is the loveliest and sweetest. It has three things that make it a perfect illustration of our Lord and savior, the shape, color, and fragrance. It's called the queen of the flowers, and it's the sweetest when it reminds you of the Lord Jesus Christ. The rose is the most common as well as the most beautiful of all the flowers. You find it wherever you go, in all countries and in all places, in fact it is the universal flower. It belongs to everybody in this aspect it resembles Christ.

Christ is common which means belonging to or shared alike. God is always here for all of us. He is there for the peasant and the prince, the poor and the rich, from the child to the full-grown woman or man. He belongs to all nations. Who cannot say, "the Lord Jesus Christ is my savior?" I claim him as my own. Christ character was marked not only by manliness, also what we call sweetness, he had all firmness of a man, but the tenderness of a woman, this is the reason for the comparison of Christ to the rose. The stem of the rose has thorns that will stick, stretch, or cut if not careful, but it's pedals are delicate, you can barely touch them and they will fall off, which helps you see the male and female represented in the flower. He also calls himself The Lily of The Valley.

This title is intended to teach us. The Lily of The Valley is the flower that is known by a name you all will remember. It is graceful with pretty little white bells arranged in a row on a tapering stalk. It appears to hide itself modestly under the shade of its broad green leaves. Now why is it thus chosen? Partly because the lily is of a beautiful white color and represents purity. You know how pure the Lord Jesus Christ is. Never at any time did he think or say or do anything that was wrong as a baby, as a child, or as a man. He was absolutely free from fault.

The lily of the valley has its drooping head. It retires behind the shade of its broad green leaves instead of thrusting itself forwards. This may be taken as an emblem of lowliness or humility so it will serve to remind us of the Lord Jesus Christ. Just a few things the Lord portrayed himself as. Now these verses start the chapter on the man.

John 4:1-4 When therefore the Lord knew how the Pharisees had heard that Jesus made and baptized more disciples than John. 2-Though Jesus himself baptized not, but his disciples. 3-He left Judea and departed again into Galilee 4-And he must need to go through Samaria.

In light of this text our subject and the directive of this chapter, that you may have a clear view of what is going on in this text. I'll give a brief description of what Jesus is doing. Now Jesus left Judea because the Pharisees were enraged against him for his teaching. The Pharisees were a stickler for the law but could not keep it themselves. Jesus was a threat to their leadership. Jesus was the light of the world and wherever he went darkness was exposed and expelled. For that reason, they sought to get rid of him.

Jesus had more work that needed to be done so he left the country to escape what the Pharisees had design for him. He went where he was less provoking. Now Jesus left not because he was afraid but because his time had not yet come. This means the time fixed in the counsels of God, the Old Testament prophecies, for the Messiah to be cut off, he had not finished his testimony and therefore would not surrender or expose himself. He also knew his disciples were not able to bare hardships at this time, therefore he would not expose them to it.

Hereby he gives an example to his own rule when they persecute you in one city, then flee to another. We are not called to suffer when we can avoid it without sin so we may not change for our own preservation, or our religion and yet we may change our place. As Jesus did, he secured himself by leaving for the direction and encouragement of others. In the King James Version of the bible the gospel of St. John chapter four and the fourth verse it said he needs to go through Samaria. The way through Samaria was the shortest distance to Galilee, there was another way that Jesus could have gone but that way was much longer, which would not have made much sense, seeing that at that time they did most of their travel by foot. Unless this woman would have been in that direction and in that case, I know he would have gone that way, because wherever there is a need. Jesus will be there and would not hesitate to go the extra miles for someone in need and he want you to know that he doesn't mine making a special trip just for you as he did for this Samaritan woman whenever there is a need Jesus will be there. Which is how we ought to be when it comes to helping others.

Jesus is a God that meets his people needs. Jesus knew that this Samaritan woman, would be there and that she needed help, this was an opportunity that he would not miss unlike some of us we let so many great opportunities just pass us by. Because we are not obedient to the spirit when he speaks to us or just don't listen or pay attention for the time to help in getting people to Christ. In this verse the word (needs) is a general term referring to what a person requires to achieve and maintain health and wellbeing a necessity or a thing, we must have.

From Brokenness to Wholeness

Jesus Will Supply Our Needs

Jesus will meet you where you are to get you to where you need to be. Jesus having all power, and knowledge is always ready to help those that genuinely seek him. There are times in our lives when we are in certain situation of deep pain and hurt that we can't talk to people are even to God but we connect with him on a deeper level from our heart and soul we reach out and cry out to God to help us, not always with words, but we serve a God that knows our every thought and desires and will come to our rescue, and then there are times we confuse our needs with our wants many of us don't really know what we need when it comes to what is best for us. But there is away for us to know and that is to surrender to the will of God and just do what he says do and that will make our lives a whole lot better.

But my God shall supply all your needs according to his riches in glory by Christ Jesus. Philippians 4:19

Keep in mind that God doesn't just supply our needs he provides everything for us according to his riches in glory, its humanly impossible to fathom the depth and range of God's glorious treasury his resources are without limits. He is the creator and owner of all things. All that we have belong to him, so how do we make a withdrawal from God's account when we need resources, we take it up with Jesus and whatever you need you shall have for the Lord is here for you. He lets you know in his word that he will supply your needs and not only your physical needs but spiritual and emotional. In any situation or circumstance God is able to do all things there is nothing that's too hard for God if you allow him to do it for you.

God supply needs that we don't even know we have this brought to mind the scripture from Genesis 2:18, when Adam was in the garden before God made the woman Adam was so happy and satisfied with God, that he didn't know he had a need, it was God that said it's not good that man should be alone , and God that gave him someone to commune with. If God will supply needs that we don't even know we have, I know he will give us what we go to him in prayer and ask him for this is needs not wants but God is so good, if we are trying to live a holy life. He will even give us some of the things we want and things that's in his will because we can ask for some crazy things and expect God to give them to us. God is a God of order and not a God of confusion.

We are talking about supplying our needs. And we must understand who God is and when we go to God be real open honest and expecting God to give us what we need according to his riches in glory not according to what we think because we don't have a clue about the riches of God. We can't beat God giving God takes whatever is done to his people, as done to himself and will repay them good and bad so its important that we help others with good and not bad because it's coming back. We are always indebted to God because he is always repaying our debts, we may do what we can with what we have but God always have our backs when we are invested in him, his people, and his work.

Testimony

God has always been there for me, even when I didn't know he was thee through dangers seen and unseen. When I did all kind of crazy things in my life, not even realizing or taking into consideration that God was there with me or that he had a special purpose for my life. Because I didn't feel that there was anything special about me at all or that I had any special talents to speak of. I used to say that I was the black sheep in my family, but now that I have grown up a lot in my feelings and emotions, I say that's how I felt. I loved my mom, but we were never really close, she didn't show love easily.

I don't know a lot of the things my mom went through or had to endure, I guess you could say I don't know her story. But this is my story and my journey, but without God and her there would be no me, so whatever my journey she will always be a part. My father went home to be with the Lord when I was eight years old. He was a kind loving and gentle soul a man of God he was really something else to me, this tall yellow man.

Was so kind and loving. There have been many times in my life I wished I could crawl back up into his lap and feel safe again, as I did when I was a little girl. I guess it's safe to say that I was and still is a daddy's girl. Because I have another father that found me and rescued me and he loves on me every day of my life, so I live my life now that one day I can see them both face to face, so when my journey here on earth is done this is what I am looking forward to. I want you to know a little bit about me and my journey so that you can better understand how I came to write this book that it's not just something out of the air, but a life lived, and things experienced by a real person and how God brought me through my soul gets happy thank you lord! He rescued me, he rescued me, GOD! He rescued me! Hallelujah, Hallelujah praise his most holy name.

God was steering me in the direction he wanted me to go, everything that happened to me everything that I had gone through good and bad may not have been orchestrated by God, but he used it all to get me to where he wanted me to be. I didn't know then, but I realize now that every situation, every circumstance, and everything that happen in my life was to maneuver me into the purpose God, had for my life what he had already predestined me to be. It was as if he planned my whole life out and then started me in it, so my life is a surprise to me, but not to God. There are some mistakes I was destined to make but God will always take care of his own and there is no exception.

This is not a detailed rehashing of all my hurts and dirt, but it's enough to allow you to see where this book originated from and make no mistake there has been a lot of deep hurt and pain, but you can't move forward looking back and living in the past or the pain we must allow God to heal us from whatever has us broken so that we may be whole enough to move into our purpose. God heal me enough so that I was able to move into my purpose, but he is still healing me when I make it over one hurdle, I am presented with another one that I didn't even know existed, one step at a time.

The scares of sin are deep and lasting and only God can heal you, so we are able to handle whatever hinders us from our work. His advice to believers is to cast all your cares upon him, trust in him with a firm composed mind, for he cares for you. Things that torture and distract the mind can render you unfit for duties and hinder your service for the Lord and your best remedy is cast our cares on him and to resign every event to his wise and gracious counsels. A firm belief in his divine will and counsel will calm the spirit of those who trust solely in him.

Casting all your care upon him for he careth for you. 1 Peter 5:7

From Brokenness to Wholeness

All your anxieties all your worries give them to the Lord because he means for you to throw them to him. God don't want us to carry heavy burdens, troubles, and problems he said throw them to him, he is able and always there to handle your every situation.

Jesus Waits Long for Us

Now Jacob's well was there. Jesus, therefore, being wearied with his journey, sat thus on the well; and it was about the sixth hour. John 4:6

Jesus had a purpose when he came to earth and that purpose was to save mankind. Man had fallen from grace by disobeying God and needed a savior, someone to redeem them back to God again. For those that don't know when God created mankind, he placed them in a garden called Eden. He created them in a perfect state with no sin and provided them with everything they needed. The one thing for them to not do, they were not to eat of a tree that was in the mist of the garden. Every other tree they could freely eat except for this one tree. They disobeyed God and this cause their disconnection with God.

This was also the first sin, so man needed to be restored back to God again and only God could do it. So, in the counsel of the God head it was decided that God himself would come down to earth himself to pay man's sin debt. So, a body was prepared, and God came to earth through the virgin Mary in the person of Jesus Christ, lived on earth 33 and ½ years and not only did he save mankind, but he also set the perfect examples for his people such as to how to live in peace without sin. The bible said that Jesus was wearied with his journey, wearied means to be exhausted physically or mentally tired by hard work, to be strained, fatigued or without vigor and freshness. He was wearied with his journey in other words with his travel.

On the other hand, we get physically, mentally, and emotionally worn out not of our spiritual journey but of life's journey with the toils of life on our journey there is many times things happen that wear on us. This is when we come to God for help for him to save us and start us on the right road. He waits on us to get tired of things of the world and for us to give our life to him so we can walk into the purpose he has for our lives. Jesus wants us to come to him willingly and to love him. He waits for us to see just how blessed we are to have such a loving God.

On our side he will never make us do anything but on our journey. He will wait till we come to him on our own and he is long suffering, yet he gave us all free will and he will never take that away. Jesus is in Samaria sitting on Jacob's well waiting for this woman because he knows she will be there and that she needed his help.

And now he sits on the well, and he waits for her aren't you glad he waited for you so that you could have a more fulfilling life. A life with love, purpose and meaning I know I am glad and so thankful that he didn't leave me to myself because he knew I would have ruined myself, but because he showed up for me and waited on me, my life has meaning now. I know Jesus waited on me even when I didn't even know he was waiting. He waited when my life was a wreak. He waited when I was broken and hurt. He waited when other people in my life walked off and left me, he waited, and I am not the only one he waited for.

He waited for you as well when you thought life had no meaning he waited. When you were addicted to drugs and alcohol he waited. While you chased fame, sex, money, and good times, he waited. He waited for us all to come to ourselves. He is long suffering waiting on us because it's not his will that anyone should perish but that the world through him might be saved. All of us right now should be shouting because he didn't give up on us. He waited until we could come to him and surrender our life to him.

This God that we serve went above and beyond all we can even imagine securing our safety and we take our relationship so lightly after all he did for us what an awesome God, we serve there is none like him. I don't care what other people may think, there is none like my God. And he is waiting for his people to turn from their evil ways, because he is waiting for us all so we can live with him forever. Just as the prodigal son did in Luke fifteen, he left home with this portion of his father's inheritance thinking things were going to be better. He wasted all he had on riotous living, and no one would give him anything.

From Brokenness to Wholeness

Bad things have to sometimes happen to us for us to really see what's important in life. When the prodigal son came to himself and realized that his father had more than enough, and that he was perishing with hunger. He said, "I will arise and go home to my father's house." Many of us need to come to ourselves and get up and go back to God and say to God Lord I am sorry I took you for granted. Because you have been so good to me and have always been there for me, I disregarded your word and did as I wanted, and you still waited on me please forgive me Lord and help me to totally sell out to you.

When this boy came to himself what made him say I will arise and go to my father's house? Well I am glad you asked in this text the father represent God and God is our safe place he is where we run when we are in trouble, hurting, sick, lonely, are just need someone to talk to and as parents we should always try to be a safe place for our children just as God is always there for us and even if our children leave, they will always know that there is a place that they can come back to no matter what. And as children of God even though we may wonder off from God, we know that God is so loving that we can always come back. God will forgive us. He is always a safe place for his children.

When the world has beaten us up, we can always run to God, our hiding place, our safe place of comfort healing and restoration. I know we are not God, and we fall very short in being the parents that even come close to how God is to us. We must work hard on being the best we can be when it comes to our children. First of all, we need to admit that we need God's help to be what he would have us to be as parents.

If we are honest with God, He will help us, and we can be that safe place for our children. I know many of you have messed up as parents. I am so glad that God is a God of another chance. He will help us to do better by our children. As we learn to be better, we can do better. Many of us parents have been hurt and broken and as I said earlier hurt people, hurt people. In raising our children, we mess up and don't provide that safe place for our children. It wasn't provided for us, so the viscus circle continues.

The son in the story of the prodigal knew he had a safe place to go to when he got in trouble. He said, "back at home, even the servants have enough and enough to spare, and here I am about to perish with hunger I know what I will do, I will go home and just ask my father to make me one of the hired servants." This boy knew he had made a big mistake in leaving his father's home. He didn't feel he was worthy to go back as his father's. Son, he does know that even the servants are treated well and have more than enough.

The father in this story never went looking for his

son. He waited for his son to come to himself and come home. When his son did come home the father was right there waiting for him and rejoiced at his return. God is waiting right now for someone that has wandered away from him and have ended up in a hog pin. The father is waiting patiently for you to come home. All you must do is come to yourself, repent, and go back to God. He will restore you. All of heaven will rejoice over your return.

Testimony

There are many of God's people wasting their lives on riotous living, drinking, gambling, lying, cheating, parting, and all kind of immoral acts and have just forgotten all about what the Lord have done for all his people. Was it not enough that he died for us and showed us exactly how to live? He stayed with us for thirty-three and one-half years, teaching, preaching, and preparing men to continue teaching and preparing men. It was so that all men can have a chance to live with him forever.

God is a patient God and wait a long time for his children to come home, but even God's patience wear out. I know that the world has many enticements that seems so alluring, but trust me when I tell you, it's not worth it. Can't nobody do you like the Lord. Out of all the things I have been through in my life, out of all the things I thought was enjoyment none of it amounted to a hill of beans. God is who matters. I really don't have the words that can truly and honestly express how good God is.

I wish that you would just do as the 34th Psalms verse 8 says, "O taste and see that the Lord is good." If only we would try God, he is so amazing. You would be wondering why you waited so long. I know I've been there; I haven't always been in with the Lord as I am now. Trust me when I tell you I wouldn't take nothing for my journey now. My life is so full, and I am so satisfied with the Lord.

Jesus is still waiting for so many of his people. It's not his will that they be lost. He wished that we all be saved and live with him in our new home in glory. God waited for this woman at the well. He waited for me, and he is waiting for you today. Give him a try and see if you won't be saying the same thing that I am saying. My life is so full, and I am so satisfied with the Lord.

From Brokenness to Wholeness

Jesus Is an On Time God

I've often heard it said that Jesus may not come when you want him, but he is always on time. When Jesus made it to Jacob's well and sat down the bible said it was about the sixth hour of the day which is said to be about noon time, and the Samaritan woman arrive about the same time. Now do you think that this was a coincidence, or chance meeting or divinely orchestrated by God himself. Our journey in life takes us on many different roads, some with crooks, some with steep turns, and some with winding roads. In other words, our paths are not always going to be straight easy or smooth sailing.

Life is unpredictable. troubles will come up out of nowhere and without warning. God is our compass, and he will lead and guide us in the right direction. We must follow where he leads. Just when you think there is no hope for your situation, just as he did for this woman at the well, he will be there for you. In the story of Lazarus Jesus didn't show up until Lazarus had been dead for four days, and he was still right on time.

Then said Martha unto Jesus, lord if thou hadst been here, my brother had not died: Jesus said unto her I am the resurrection, and the life he that believeth in me, though he were dead, yet shall he live; and whosoever liveth and believeth in me shall never die.

From Brokenness to Wholeness

Believest thou this? John 11:21, 25-26

Never give up on God! Many things do not work out the way we think they should, but we should remember who God is. Too many times we put God on human level with his creation when there is no comparison at all. We are just frail human beings prone to fail and make mistakes. Whereas God never fails to keep his word or to see it through. All we have to do is just trust him and believe in his word. He has given us evidence and examples which show that he never falls short of his word or his promises.

He may not do things the way we may want or think he should. But who are we? His ways are not like our ways his thoughts and ways are higher than ours. We can always trust that when he fixes somethings its fixed. The fact that Jesus does nothing just to do it and the fact that the time of day is included in the text it holds some significance. I believe the time was important in relation to what I am writing about. I will share in the next chapter titled (The Woman). But you can rest assure that he was on time for his work. To save a soul was no small thing to Jesus. Unlike we are today we let numerous opportunities pass by and miss out on a chance to bring people to Christ.

Some of us would be late for our own funeral if it wasn't for the fact that the undertakers are in charge of getting us there, LOL. But whether it was one or one million people, Jesus was and is always on time, as we should be when it comes to God's business.

I believe that many of God's people are hurting broken and in need of God's healing. And as you read this book, I want you to know that there is help for whatever you may be going through, God is a healer it makes no difference whither its physical, spiritual, or emotional whatever it is he, is able and can supply all your needs. The God that we serve is a loving and patient God that waits long for his people to come to him. He is also an on-time God all that we need is in him he supplies all our needs he waits long for us, and he is an on-time God.

From Brokenness to Wholeness

Chapter Two: The Woman

Jesus answered and said unto her if thou knewest the gift of God, and who it is that saith to thee, give me to drink; thou wouldest have asked of him, and he would have given thee living water.

The Need of a Personal Relationship

Many of God's people are missing out on a personal relationship with God having someone to lean on, someone to go to when things get really difficult or bad in their life. We all need a true support system, someone that truly understand everything you are going through, if you remember there is nothing hid from God, He know everything there is to know about you all your little dirty dirt and all your little nasty secrets, He knows so you can talk to him honestly and tell him your whole heart because he already knows anyway. The Samaritan woman arrive at the well to draw water and Jesus ask her to give him a drink. We learned in studying this test that the Jews have no dealing with the Samaritan, so Jesus being a Jew was not expected to converse with this Samaritan woman, but as we learn earlier Jesus' ways are not as ours are he has no respect of persons in other words Jesus don't pick anyone out or leave anyone out because of who they maybe, he is God. But this Samaritan woman is surprised and ask him why he ask a drink of her.

Who is a Samaritan given the situation with the

From Brokenness to Wholeness

Jews and the Samaritans? So, Jesus answers her and tells her if she knew the gift of God and who he was, she would be asking him for a drink, and he would have given her living water. Now in this conversation with Jesus and this woman, the dialog between them continues. Now the Samaritan woman tells Jesus that he has nothing to draw with, and the well is deep, so where is he going to get this living water, so she is thinking of this water from what she sees and know the physical. But what Jesus is talking about is not the physical but the spiritual. Now in order to understand the spiritual you must be spiritual.

But the natural man receveth not the things of the spirt of God: for they are foolishness unto him: neither can he know them, because they are spiritually discerned. 1 Corinthians 2:14

So, the Samaritan woman at this time, had no idea what Jesus was talking about, but she tries to figure it out, the only way she knows how, in the physical. Jesus being God and man, already knows everything there is to know about this woman. As he does with everyone, there is nothing hid from him. Whatever your problems are, your hang-ups or your traumas may be whatever you have been through. Let me save you sometime, he already knows. So, when you come to God, you can be honest and open with him. That way you can get the help you need. I know some of you may be ashamed, sad, hurting or even at the point of giving up.

I know the feeling I've been there, but God is there with you. After Jesus's struggled in prayer in the garden of Gethsemane, angels came and ministered to him. They will do the same for his people today. I believe this Samaritan woman felt all these things and more, and really wanted help for her situation. She didn't see any way out. The bible didn't say this woman was laying around with all kinds of men. Not that was she doing all kinds of immoral acts, it said she had five husbands and he who thou hast now is not thy husband.

Now some people will look at that and say that this woman was hoeing around, but that's not what I see, what I see is someone that's looking for love in all the wrong places, that didn't have all the correct information or understanding, but she was trying, and I believe that she had a desire to do the right thing, the bible didn't say the husband that you are with it said he/ man that you are with now is not yours, which could have meant that she wasn't married to that man, she had five failed marriages and was now with someone that she was not married to in Hebrews 13:4 states that marriage is honorable.

Marriage is honorable in all, and the bed undefiled: but whoremongers and adulterers God will judge. Hebrews 13:4

From Brokenness to Wholeness

I can't speak for the woman at the well, because it is not written, but speaking for myself, I just didn't want to be committing fornication, so it was marry me, or keep it moving. I wanted someone to love me to fill that void that was in my life, and I wanted to honor God in my relationships. Don't get me wrong I did a lot of wrong in my life and I am not trying to cover it up. That is just how I felt, but it was also wrong to have all those failed marriages. I was swapping the witch for the broom if you will. Instead of staying and trying to work on my first marriage, and

God showed me that and people talked about me. When people are not in your shoes, they will judge you. This is part of the reason it took me so long to write this book. I was worrying about what people were going to say. I also learned that some of the same people that were talking didn't have any room to even open their mouths. They had their own dirt and nasty secrets. I learned better, and God help me to get over worrying about what people might say. What I have gone through may help someone else. I am doing better now. I have been married now sixteen years to my real knight in shining armor.

He is the last husband I said I would talk about. He is a man of God, a pastor, teacher, preacher, husband, father, grandfather, lover, and friend. He is not perfect; he makes mistakes; he does wrong sometimes, but he love's God above all and he loves' me, and I thank

God for the blessing in my husband, and it wasn't until I got satisfied with God that this man came into my life.

It's done, all the husbands I have had its done. Till death do part us, that's it. It's finished. My husband and I, when we met, we were looking for the same thing, someone that loved God, and wanted to do ministry. We wanted to live our life together, growing together and to grow in Christ. I thank God that after all we have been through, we are doing just that. As I said we are not perfect, and we make mistakes, but we go to God to keep us on track. We are not doing anything on our own, it's God, that's keeping us and leading us, and showing us what to do and how to do it.

When troubles come up in our life, we have someone we can go to that knows how to fix whatever it is. God knows how to turn your mess into miracles and to work all things out for your good, even the bad. We all have things that we need to get past, or be delivered from, strong holds that have been built up in our lives from childhood. Satan tries to put stumbling blocks in your life early to derail you from your purpose. It works in a lot of people lives and have them crippled their whole life and can't move forward. So many people are walking around broken and hurting from past experiences. People put on a façade and masquerade as if all is well but are in need of help

From Brokenness to Wholeness

and healing and especially women.

You know women are good at hiding their feelings and covering up their hurt and acting as if all is well. When they are broken on the inside. I believe the woman at the well name wasn't mentioned because this Samaritan woman could be any woman. Not the fact that she had had five husbands, but that's she was broken, wounded, and hurting. Well, you may ask, how do I know so much about this woman?

Testimony

Well, I am this woman. How am I this woman? When I read this story of the woman at the well, I was amazed that my story was in the bible. I don't know this Samaritan woman's full story, only what's written and what the Holy Spirit has revealed to me through my own story. Helping me, healing me, and making me whole. I will be open and honest about my life so that someone maybe helped. I was ashamed of all the mistakes. I didn't really want anyone to know.

But we serve such a good, wonderful, and merciful God. He has helped me to overcome worrying about what people think. And use the things I've been through to help someone else find their healing.

So just let me snatch the Band-Aid off and go on and put this out there. I have been married many times. I am sure if you know the story of the woman at the well. You can see why I said that she was I. That's my story in the bible. All I wanted was to have a happy home and marriage, someone that loved me. So, my journey begins.

My first marriage was at the age of fifteen. I thought he was my knight in shining armor. He would rescue me from a life I thought was hard and unfair. I would soon wish for this life again. After a while of being with the man I thought loved me above all, I found that he was a mean womanizer. These are things I wouldn't be saying if they weren't true. I'm sure you have heard it said that the proof is in the pudding, but I lately heard someone else say the proof is in the eating of the pudding.

In other words, there is really no way of knowing what's in the pudding if you haven't tried it. The proof in that pudding was that the man that I married is now the father of over twenty children by I don't know how many women. Don't worry I will not bore you with details and hurts from all these marriages, just the first and the last. The others were very fleeting.

On my journey to find the love I lost when I lost my father, I also sought the love I never got from my mother. I was in a cycle of looking for love and acceptance in all the wrong people. This only led me to more hurt, pain, disappointment, abuse, mistreatment, and men using me. The web of the devil was weaved for my destruction. But God. I will tell you now, you don't have to wait till the end of the story. I always did like my desert before the meal. What the devil meant for my bad, God used it for my good.

The woman at the well, this woman was parched, in poverty, and had no purpose. Parched because she came for water, but in the spiritual, she was empty on the inside. God placed an emptiness in all his people heart that can only be filled or satisfied by him. She was also poor and had to come to the well to get water for herself. We know she was poor, because she drew her own water, and the wealthy sent servants to draw water for them. I think this woman didn't really have full knowledge or understanding of what she was doing. But I do believe.

She was trying to figure it all out, life and relationships. She didn't have a purpose why she was doing what she was doing. This woman's life parallels with mine. I was thirsty for what was missing in my life, and I thought it was the love of a man that was missing. I didn't understand or know about the void that God places inside his people to be filled by him.

He has also set eternity in the hearts of men; Ecclesiastes 3:11 (b) NIV

I thought I was looking for the love I lost in my natural father, because he was the picture I had of real love. Now that I can see clearly, and God have opened my spiritual eyes I know that there is a much bigger reason for my search and longings that was in my life. It was God, drawing me to him and to the only love that could give me what I truly needed. He is the only one that can love me like I needed to be loved. There was no reason to look to anyone else for that love. It's only found in Christ. Now I can say to all of the men that were in my life that, "I am sorry. Sorry because I expected them to give me what they didn't have in them to give."

We will one day be able to give that love, when we see God, we will be able to love as he does. Now I need to talk a little bit about what Jesus was doing to get this woman to understand what he was saying to her. He needed her to see that she was in the physical but needed be in this spiritual. This is how she would know what Jesus was talking about. And as I studied, I came across the method that Jesus used in bringing this woman to Christ.

And if we use this method, we too can bring people to Christ, and also into a better relationship. There is always room for improvement in our relationships with God because we are learning and growing everyday of our life. We need a good relationship with the Lord, because its him that will carry our cares for us. The Samaritan woman needed such a relationship. This woman's conscience needed to be awakened. For that to happen, Jesus had to open

From Brokenness to Wholeness

the wound of guilt within her so that she could more easily comprehend the remedy of God's grace. This is the method that Jesus used dealing with this woman's soul. We must first be made weary and heavy laden under the burden of sin, and then brought to Christ for rest.

We must first be pricked in the heart and then healed. This is the course of spiritual physics and if we proceed not in this order we begin at the wrong end. Now that we know what Jesus is doing and how he is doing it. Let's look at this well.

The woman saith unto him Sir, thou hast nothing to draw with, and the well is deep: from whence then hast that living water? John 4:11

In the text this deep well is a metaphor in the spiritual of her brokenness. It's the set of her woundedness, even though it didn't show on the outside. She was wounded and hurting, so she tells Jesus that this well is deep and he didn't have anything to draw with. Not knowing that Jesus was already drawing her out. He tells her if you knew the gift of God and who it is that ask her for a drink, she would be asking him for a drink. Now this is to further draw on her curiosity to know more.

What, this woman is really saying, is I am so broken, and my wounds are so deep, you can't help, me. You can't even get to them because they are so deep. In other words, my wounds are such that are unreachable. You can't help me in this situation that I am in. I have pushed them down deep so I can cope with life. The abuse, I pushed it down, the cruelty, I pushed it down, the mistreatment, I pushed it down, the beatings, I pushed it down, the rape, I pushed it down, the molestation, I pushed it down, I pushed it all the way down and that's why you cannot help me. This well is deep, and you have nothing to draw with.

But she didn't know who she was talking to. She wasn't talking to an ordinary man. She was talking to the most high God, Jesus the Christ. Many of God's people spend their whole life living with hurt, abuse, and traumas that have happen. To them in their life many of God's women haven't had anyone to protect them. The men in their lives that were there to protect them, were the very ones that were hurting them. They couldn't tell, or talk about it, or ask for help. They just stuffed it down deep to survive. Women put on a façade, and walk around with smiles on their faces, when they are broken on the inside. But there is help. I found it in the pages of God's word. There is power and life in the word of God.

From Brokenness to Wholeness

Chapter Three: The Message

Whosoever drinketh of this water shall thirst again: But whosoever drinketh of the water that I shall give him shall never thirst; but the water that I shall give him shall be in him a well of water springing up into everlasting life. John 4:13 (b), 14

This woman now wants to know from Jesus where he is going to get this water he is talking about. She is still trying to figure it out, so she compares the water that Jesus is offering to the water at Jacob's well. But Jesus let's her know that there is no comparison, that whoever drink the water that he shall give shall never thirst again, and he compares it to a well of water springing up into everlasting life. Jesus offers this woman lasting satisfaction through his living water. It's important that you understand that the living water is a metaphor for the Holy Spirt, when people get saved, the Holy Spirit comes and lives inside of his people, those that have accepted him as their personal Lord and savior,

To be saved means to believe in your heart and confess with your mouth that Jesus came to earth, born of a virgin named Mary, lived for thirty-three and a half years, went to the cross and gave his life for his people sins, died, and was buried and the third day rose again from the died. This is the message that is being preached today, the same message that the people that are saved share with others as often as they have the opportunity to. The Holy Spirit help's his people to live a holy life, he also has the true knowledge of God, who teach his people God's will, guide, direct and reveals God's character by Jesus sacrificial love for his people.

The Holy Spirit give's his people an intimate relationship with God and brings them closer with him. The Holy Spirit furnish the believer with a firm foundation of hope and overflowing fountain of joy, we are saved, filled, sealed, and sanctified through the power of the Holy Spirit, the Christians life is an ongoing process of becoming holy through sanctification. And once we've been truly saved it's a done deal, we are in the body of Christ forever. He said in his word in (Philippians 1:6)

Being confident of this very thing, that he which hath begun a good work in you will perform it until the day of Jesus Christ.

God will not save his people and lose them, he is not that kind of God, to leave things unfinished. The Holy Spirit is on his job twenty-four seven to make sure that God's people get the right information. He bears witness to the truth, when we hear the word being preached or taught, he let us know that its truth. God's message is what save souls, what change lives, and what make life worth living, we know why we are here and what to do while we are here, and if that is not clear to you yet, just keep reading and if it's not clear by the end of this book then go back to the beginning, pray and ask God to give you insight, to open up your spiritual understanding. You know in God's word, Matthew 6:33 (KJV) it states.

But seek ye first the kingdom of God, and his righteousness, and all these things shall be added unto you.

We chase after things in this life, that we think will satisfy us, but if the truth be told, nothing in this life last forever, possessions, relationships and even desires all fade away and feeling change like the wind. Even when we obtain the things that we've been chasing after, the satisfaction will only last for a little while, then it gone, no matter the amount of money, things, desires, or how good we think our relationships, are everything must come to an end.

The only thing that will last forever is our relationship with God, and the sad part about that is not that this other stuff doesn't last, but that we treat our relationship with God as if it's the least important. Again, there is a void in all of our lives that can only be filled or satisfied by God. Jesus offers this woman lasting satisfaction through his living water, and not only is the offer for this woman but it's for all people today, and if you have not excepted JESUS, as your personal savior, please stop right now and invite him into your heart, he can make all things new in your life, this is the most important decision you will ever make in your life, he can turn your life around, no matter how bad you think things are, he is able, he raised the dead, I know he can fix whatever is going on in your life, take a break and talk to him right now, he is right there with you just waiting for you to ask him in.

Behold, I stand at the door, and knock: if any man hears my voice, and open the door, I will come into him, and will sup with him, and he with me. Revelation 3:20 (KJV)

The message of God is clear and plain for those that want a life in him. This world offers many things, none of which can fully satisfy the longings of the soul. But God, gives us real satisfaction. Our physical bodies will always be craving the physical things of this world, which is why it's so important that we have God's living water, the Holy Spirit to keep the flesh under control. The message we share is that we need the Holy Spirit living inside of us so that we may live the abundant life, and money is not what gives us that abundant life, it is the Holy Spirit working through us, to reach and touch other lives, so they too can experience that abundant life, if each one reach one, then we all will have the opportunity to live that abundant life, to experience God in a more intimate way, through his message.

The infirmities of our bodies in this present state, they are still needy and ever craving, our physical bodies must be kept under submission to the spirit, which is why the bible teaches that we must crucify daily our flesh. Life is like a fire or lamp, which will soon go out, without continual supplies of fuel and oil. The imperfections of all our comforts in this world are not lasting, nor will our satisfaction in them remain. Whatever waters of comforts we drink from we shall thirst again. We must always be coming up with something new to quince our thirst and satisfy our cravings. We are never fully satisfied without the Holy Spirit living inside of us, our helper is always on alert to help us to control our flesh, our craving and desires through the convictions and power of the Holy Spirit, believers will not indulge in the sinful acts of the flesh.

It's the Spirit work to guide to good character by intimating God, that we behave as he does, and to led us to our purpose, to work towards, or set our sights on heaven, to strive for our end. The Holy Spirit lives inside all believers, he fills your very being that lets you know everything will be alright in every situation through the good and the bad, he gives assurance of salvation you don't have to wonder where you will spend eternity, and safety, he will always take care of us no matter what, we are covered under his blood and sanity he will keep you in perfect peace who's mind is stayed on him. He is our counselor. The Holy Spirit is simply God's way of reconciling man back to himself, after the fall in the garden the fellowship between God and man needed to be restored, after the fall, man died spiritually, therefore losing their connection with God. This is all a part of God's plan to restore man again, for he foreknew what would happen and that he had to have a way to set things right again. This message of living water or the Holy Spirit, is God's way of fixing what man messed up. And it's so important that we keep telling the story of Jesus birth, death, and resurrection so that others might be saved. And once we have the message and believer the message and are saved then it's time to move into the purpose that God have for his children life.

This woman left her water pots and ran into the city to tell, whoever would listen, come see a man, who told me all I ever did she found her purpose, what she needed to be doing and why she needed to do it. The ministry, the work God has for his people to do. God's general will and his specific will, the general will is for everyone to be saved and his specific will is what God want each individual to do.

Testimony

I didn't know or understand it when God filled me, but he gave me everything I needed, when he filled me with his precious Holy Spirit, in that instance there was no more feelings of despair or feeling so needy, I had all I needed in him, I knew from that day on that I would be alright and that I would be able to handle whatever came my way because I had a helper, that was always there to help me in my time of need. What I experienced that day gave new meaning to the scripture, greater is he that is in me, than he that is in the world. Without a doubt I am a new creation in Christ Jesus, my life will never be the same, I am forever changed, and I thank God for changing me.

The Ministry

The woman then left her water pots, and went her way into the city and saith to the men come see a man which told me all things that ever I did: is not this the Christ? John 4:28-29

This woman left her water pots because she was taken up with something more important, of telling the good news, come see a Man she wanted them to experience what she had experience, the awesome power of Jesus Christ and the fact that he knew everything there was to know about her, this was a real encounter with God, and it made a lasting impression on her, and changed her life forever. Once people have a real encounter with Jesus their life will change for the better. Jesus' meeting with this Samaritan woman was not a coincidence but rather a predestined meeting that was going to take place. Earlier in the text Jesus said he had a need to go through Samaria, and his need came out of the fact that this Samaritan woman would be there, and she was in need and he was the only one that could attend her needs. The message of Jesus Christ has the power to reach way down and save even the worst of sinner. The Samaritan woman had undergone an inward transformation, her heart had been changed and she was ready to begin her new life in Christ Jesus, to share the good news, to get others to just hear the word because it has a drawing power all of its own.

She wanted her friends and neighbors to be acquainted with Jesus, she became an apostle, she went out an example of impurity and returned a teacher of Evangelical truth, and she invited them to come and see Jesus, not only to come and look upon him for a show, but come and converse with him, come and hear his words of wisdom as she had done. Then she tells them plainly what induced her to admire him, he told her that which none knew but God and her own conscience.

There were two things that affected her, first the extent of his knowledge and second, the power of his words. This made a great impression upon her that he told her, her secret sins. Is not this the Christ? Don't ever think that anything is hid from God, he knows all. These men didn't send for Jesus to come to them, but they went to where he was, out of the earnestness of their desire to see him, those that will know Christ must put themselves in a place and position to know him.

Go ye therefore and teach all nations, baptizing them in the name of the father and of the son and of the Holy Ghost. Teaching them to observe all things whatsoever I have commanded you: and, Lo I am with you always, even unto the ends of the world. Amen. Matthew 28:19-20

God has given every believer a ministry, and if you have never figured out what God's specific will for your life, is his general will for all his people is to be, saved and then agents of reconciliation to help others come to Christ through his message. We must go, teach the message, and that people may be saved, and then baptize God's people, we will never be alone, He promise to be with us, till the end of time. This woman's life was changed, and you can tell that by her action, she was no longer concerned about drawing water, no longer concerned about her own business, but now she is concerned about God's business. Just as Jesus was so taken up with his father's business that he forgot his business of eating as a matter of fact he said that the will of his father was his meat and drink.

God has work for all his children and that's your ministry, and there is plenty of work to be done, no one's specific work is the same in its own way because

From Brokenness to Wholeness

God use who you are and the talents, he put in you to his glory. We must allow God to heal us of all our pains and hurt of the past so that we can do the work of ministry.

Now I have given you all the tools your need to lead to your healing and all that's left is for you to give your hurts and pain to the King of kings, he is able to heal you, there is nothing too hard for God. I have shown you through this Samaritan woman's life and my own, how it's done, this woman was healed from all her deep hurts and so was I, he is still healing me, and we both was brought closer to God through our own experience. Now you have an example of what to do to be whole. God is a healer of whatever is broken in you, he can make you whole, if you would just trust him with your life. This woman was in poverty, in pain and parched, this was her condition and so was I, but Jesus made a special trip just for her, and just for me and he will make a special trip just for you, he is just that kind of God there is none like him, none that can do what he do he is an awesome God.

God has given every believer a ministry and if you have never figured out what God's specific will for your life, is his general will for all his people is to be agents of reconciliation, to help others come to Christ through his message. We must go, teach, and baptize God's people, go where? His words said into all nations now we may not be able to literally or physically, but his word can go where we can't if each one, teach one then the word will travel to all nations, and then teach.

Say's study to show thyself approved unto God, a workman that needeth not to be ashamed, rightly dividing the word of truth. 2 Timothy 2:15

Which means we must prepare ourselves to be able to teach, if this is our calling, if not we should study God's word so we can live by it, but we can still share the good news of Jesus Christ. His death burial and resurrection and baptize and again there are those that have been called to do this work. This is just an outward expression showing that we believe in Jesus Christ as Lord and savior, and our new life in Christ.

Healing

Healing is the process of making or becoming sound or healthy again, it's the personal experience of transcending suffering and transforming to wholeness. There are many types of illness, first of all there is physical illness, in the body and then there is mental, dealing with the mind and then you have emotional, deal with the feeling, then there is spiritual, which deals with the soul, if a person is spiritually whole or well, that will help with all other illness, you can rely heavily on your spiritual health to help with you emotions your mental and your physical health. Which makes your spiritual health the most important because not only does it help in this life but the life after death teaches us.

And with his stripes we are healed. Isaiah 53:5 (d)

The price for your healing was paid in full by Jesus Christ on the cross, you don't pay for a product twice, by his stripes we are healed, that Christ not only came to save us from sin, but he came to make us whole. Healing in case any part of our bodies becomes sick. The words we are healed are in the past tense meaning that our healing has been fully secured on the cross by Christ 2000 years ago. It, therefore, means we are not praying for Christ to heal us but to receive healing. Christ had already secured it for us. We do not pray for victory but pray from victory to victory. My dear sisters and brothers, live with this understanding that your sickness whatever it is, or the name of it maybe, its already healed by God.

What remains is for you to claim your healing over that sickness. Now I need you to understand that there may be some illness that God don't heal on this side, which don't mean that he is not going to heal them, just not on this side. Sometimes God remove the illness, and then other times he moves the person. Don't ask me why. I don't claim to know why God do what he does. He is God, and dose what he wants to do, but I do believe that one day we will understand it all.

I had a friend that was sick with cancer, and she had fought it for a long time. Praise God through it all and when she got down really sick, she sent me a message. She wanted me to share it with the church, and that message was, "sometimes God claims the storms in our life, but then other times he claims the child in the storm." So don't say I prayed, and God didn't heal me, because it's not over till God say it's over. Never forget he is God. He knows all things, and he knows what's best in every situation, even if we don't understand. Paul prayed three times that God would remove the thorn from his flesh.

No one really knows what the thorn was. It could have been an illness. Whatever it was it was bothering him enough for him to ask God to remove it. God didn't. This thorn was given to him by Satan, but God told him that his grace was sufficient for him. This was what God used in Paul life, to keep him humble. So why does God do the things he does? We may not know or understand, but one thing we do know is that it's for our own good.

And we know that all things work together for good to them that love God, to them who are the called according to his purpose. Romans 8:28

We will encounter many situations in life, some good and some bad but weather good or bad God will use them for our good, some way, somehow, we don't have to worry God is in control and he is working it out for you, just think about what he went through for you and me, what a sacrifice! That he gave. Jesus was flogged 39 times, with one of many torturing tools of the Roman soldiers. Therefore, the price of our healing was paid in full by Christ, on the cross. Receive it in the name of Jesus. It's not God will that we be broken and hurting. It is his will that we be healthy, whole, happy and in a place to give him praise for all the many wonderful blessing that he has given to his people.

When people are in a good place with Christ, they really don't have time for things that are not going to advance the kingdom. If you remember, I said that our mental is a part of our health as well. It's so important that we guard our minds. Philippians 4:8 teaches us to think on good and positive things. In other words, make a point not to think on garbage, things that will make you feel bad and bring you down. Get rid of all stinking thinking.

Finally, brethren, whatsoever things are true, whatsoever things are honest, whatsoever things are just, whatsoever things are pure, whatsoever things are lovely, whatsoever things are of a good report; if there be any virtue, and if there be any praise, think on these things. Philippians 4:8

Our minds are where we make decisions of what

to do and choices between right and wrong, it's very important that we keep our mind in a spiritual state, so that we can make good decisions and pure choices. And if we are to have people to think well of us and be a good example for others, we must be honest and truthful in our words and engagements and decent in our behavior and in all our dealings. If our bodies, emotions, mental and spiritual <u>wellbeing</u> is going to be healthy then we must have a close relationship with God, and our minds stayed on him.

If we do that then we can have the peace of God, which passed all understanding, these are essential tools to have when things go wrong with our health, so that our bodies can recover. God is so awesome in all he has done is his creation, everything he fashioned he put rejuvenation, in itself all vegetation, animals, and human have what is needed for healing and reproduction built, in itself, what an awesome God we serve. And still there is so much we don't know and understand, we can learn something new every day till the day we die and still not know all the mysteries in God's creation. Our healing is already secured in Christ, he left nothing out in planning and preparation for our wellbeing, all that we have already been supplied, all we need to do is to learn how to access it. He also equipped the believer with the Holy Spirit, to lead and guide you and to bring to your remembrance when you need it the Holy Spirit also will assist us in staying well if we will listen and pay attention to his leading the Holy Spirit have many functions in aiding God's people, God left nothing out. We are covered in all aspects of our life, God made sure we had everything we would need, such a loving God, he made sure all the bases were covered, he wanted to make sure that the way was clear for us to make it safely home, Yes God, is a healer.

But the Comforter, which is the Holy Ghost, whom the Father will send in my name, he shall teach you all things, and bring all things to your remembrance, whatsoever I have said unto you. John 14:26

The process the woman at the well went through to get from Mersey to ministry was quite unique. So, this woman's conscience needed to be awakened. For that to happen, Jesus had to open the wound of guilt within her. She could more easily comprehend the remedy by grace. This is the method that Jesus used in dealing with this woman's soul. People must first be made weary and heavy laden under the burden of sin, and then brought to Christ for rest, first pricked to the heart and then healed, this is the course of spiritual physic, a great way to bring people to Christ, and if good enough for Christ, I know it's good enough for us. The woman at the well got her healing and was better for it and then able to walk into her purpose.

No one can heal you like God can. It's him that

gives the doctors the ability and know how, to do what they do. To help his people in their healing. God is indeed a healer. He has healed me many times and, in many ways, sick in my body, sick in my mind, sick in my emotions, and yes sick spiritually. He is my healer. I am so grateful, so grateful, to God, without him I don't know where I would be right now. He changed me and changed my life. I really feel as if I am somebody because I now know that God loves me and that I am important to him.

Whatever I may go through in this life it's okay because I am loved. I look forward to my life with my Lord and savior, so the hard times, the ups and the down's God will help me through, everything is alright. My God have my back and that I know from experience. The things I go through here don't compare to what God went through for me and all people. I am living this life to live again. Once this life is over here on earth, I have a home with God. There will be no more suffering, no more crying, no more dying, no more disappointment, no more pain, no more sickness.

No more mean, evil, and hateful people. No more jealousy no more selflessness, no more people setting traps and digging ditches for you, no more envy and mistreatment, all these things will have passed away. There will be only joy, peace, love, happiness and praising God, all the time. He has prepared all things here on earth for us and life after death. Our healing is already secured in him already fixed and made possible by him. We praise God for who he is because the God that he is, so loved us that he gave his son and his son gave his life to make things right for his people, so they could live with him forever.

Health

Health is a state of complete physical, mental, emotional, spiritual, and social well-being. It's not merely the absence of disease or infirmity. It's not merely the state of being free from illness or injury. Good health begins with a change of heart and a transformed mind. As children of God, unless we stay connected to the true vine, which is Jesus Christ, where our healing, health, and wholeness lye, we will not experience a life of health first things first. Seek ye first the kingdom of God and all his righteousness and everything else will be added unto you.

But seek ye first the kingdom of God, and his righteousness; and all these things shall be added unto you. Matthew 6:33

We must make heaven our end and holiness as our way. The best way to be comfortably provided for in this world, is to be most intent upon another world! Look to the things of God, always put him first and we won't have to worry about our well-being, God will supply all our needs according to his riches in glory.

The way to stay healthy is to remember to put God, and the things of God, first. I tried for years doing it my way, and it never worked out until I surrendered to God's ways. My life is not perfect, and I still make mistakes and do wrong on occasion. God is still working on me, but I wouldn't take nothing for my journey now. My life is so much better than it was before, and not just with material things. What's important to me is my relationship with God. I learn to love him and to put him first in my life. He is the best thing that ever happen to me, come what will or may. God is my life without him my life would have no reason. Everything centers around him. He makes my life worth living.

When I wake up in the mornings my life is about him, even if I don't pray right away, it's still about him. Everything in my life works because of him, there is a feeling of freedom and joy that cannot be explained with mere words, the best way that I can explain it is, it makes me feel like shouting, like running, like just giving God some praise! The woman at the well moved from emotional, mental, and spiritual illness to healing and then health from her encounter with Jesus, and that's what is missing in a lot of people life, and for some reason people don't want to admit that they haven't had that encounter with God.

It's nothing to be ashamed of, for many years of

my life I wouldn't admit it either, until I actually did have a real encounter with him and my life was changed forever, but don't wait like I did, go to him and ask him to help you, to heal you, so you can be of use to him and his cause, the woman at the well after her encounter with Jesus, left her water pot and went into the city and told the men come see a man who told me everything that I ever did, and so did I every sense my encounter I have been telling people just how good God is, how he came to earth by way of a virgin name Mary lived and walked the earth 32 and ½ years, healing the sick, giving sight to the blind, making the lame to walk, making the deaf to hear, and raising the dead, just telling the good news of our Lord and savior Jesus Christ, the one who hung bleed and died for our sins.

There is a saying (You don't know what you got, until it's gone). Our health is very important, it's a gift from God, we really need to learn how to appreciate it, and be thankful for everything in our lives, but we take being healthy for granted until we lose our health, we don't appreciate having the activity of our limbs, because we feel as if we will always have it. Just getting dressed or doing the everyday things we normally do, simple things that we never thought that we would need help with or wouldn't be able to do. You don't know, but God know the things you will have to endure, and if you will still praise him and keep on lifting him up, in spite of whatever our situation is.

You don't know how you will handle a situation until you are faced with it. I woke up one morning with a word from the Lord, and I thought it was God giving me a message to preach, I jumped up to write it down so that I wouldn't forget it and the word was, (it's not the hurt or the pain but the result that it will bring) This was in the year 2010, this same year I tested positive for Lupus and RA which is Rheumatoid Arthritis, I can't explain the process of my illness, but I ended up in a wheel chair.

My entire body was inflamed, and my joints was becoming deformed before my eyes, I could not walk without help, I couldn't even bathe myself. I remember crying as my baby daughter gave me a bath, because I couldn't do it myself. She tried to console me by saying, mom it's going to be alright. My body was in so much pain as I waited to see a Rheumatologist. My body locked up; I was almost totally immobile. I kept on remembering what the Lord had said to me that morning. I realized that it wasn't a sermon that God was giving me but a testimony. He was preparing me for what I was about to go through. There is no cure for what I have, so I live with this disease every day.

I give God the praise and I realized that this was God answering my prayer. I remembered standing at the alter and asking God to keep me. I was tired of being up and down, in and out in my relationship with him and this illness keeps me. It keeps me humble. It keeps me looking to God, and it keeps me focused on my ministry. God knows me way better than I know myself. He knew that I meant what I said and the God that I serve, don't half do anything. Do I miss being able to do a lot of the things I use to be able to do, yes, I do. I love God for what he allowed to happen in my life because he is working it out for my good.

This is making me better so that's just fine with me it's what I want, to please God, don't take your health for granted, don't take the blessing of God's gift of good health for granted. It can be gone just that quick, I am not sad about my situation. I have peace with God, and this is only for a season. One of these days I will get to go home and be with the Lord, and I will be whole physically again and totally whole in every way. To God be the glory for all he has done.

Wholeness

Wholeness is the state of being unbroken or undamaged, undivided, totality with nothing wanting. Wholeness is defined simply as the one thing that remains the same, even when everything else is changing. That one thing is actually not a thing, but a person, God. Healing makes you well; disease and problems will stop you from being healthy. Only wholeness will allow you to move forward, fully repaired, and rebuilt. If you are saved, you find that wholeness within yourself. You can stop looking for another person and relying on others to fill or complete you. You have all you need inside of you. God placed a void in all his children that can only be filled by him and only him. When Jesus healed the ten lepers only one came back to thank Jesus and to give him praise. That's because nine was healed, but only on was made whole.

And Jesus answering said, were there not ten cleansed? But where are the nine? There are not found that returned to give glory to God, save this stranger, and he said unto him, Arise, go thy way: they faith hath made thee whole. Luke 17;17-19

The nine was healed, but the one that came back to give Jesus' praise was made whole. We all can be made whole in Christ, in mind, body, and spirit. Jesus went away so that he could send the Holy Spirit, the comforter to live inside of us. It leads and guide us into all truth. The Holy Spirit is our protection from the evils of this world, but we must listen and pay attention to his leadings and follow his directions. Being complete and whole, the Holy Spirit gives you the assurance all believers need on this Christian journey. The enemy will come up against you to try to stop you in whatever you are doing for the Lord.

From Brokenness to Wholeness

So, you need to know, that you know, you are safe in Christ, so he can't shake your faith. When you have been made whole in Christ, everything is alright, and that's not to say that you won't have any problems, as a matter of fact, if you don't have any problems then something is really wrong, but the Holy Spirit in you will help you handle whatever come's your way, he is the living water that's always overflowing and always bubbling up into everlasting life.

Spiritual wholeness does not mean that there will not be any trouble or problems in your life. It's to have the love, joy, and peace of the Lord, in the mist of your storms. In this life every day is not going to be sunshine. Things are not going to go the way you may want them to all the time. The bible teaches that in this life we will have our share of trials and tribulations. One thing you can always count on is that God is always there for you, no matter what you must face.

Enjoying spiritual wholeness is not the absence of troubles. It is keeping your joy and peace in the mist of troubles. There is nothing like just knowing everything is going to be alright when troubles come. When hard times come, when the bills are more than the money, when no one is happy with you, you still feeling safe and satisfied in Christ. You know he is going to work whatever it is out, for your good. The woman at the well was made whole at the end of her conversation and encounter with Jesus. She dropped her water pots and went into the city to tell the men about her encounter with Jesus. Jesus had taken care of her problems and now she wanted to do the work of the Lord, and it will be the same for his people today. If we take care of God's business, he will take care of ours. I can truly say that doing the will of the Father, everything just seems to fall in place. There is such comfort and peace in being whole in Christ, it makes your burdens lighter, your stress level is much lower, and it's much easier just to keep a smile on your face.

From Brokenness to Wholeness

Note from the Author

1 Corinthians 6:18 Flee fornication. Every sin that a man doeth is without the body; but he that committeth fornication sinneth against his own body.

I must be very honest with you. It might not be easy to hear if you are not a truth hearer. I can't apologize for the truth of the word of God. in truth, somethings we bring on ourselves. It's because of our own disobedience, the bible teaches us that sexual sins are sins against our own body. In other words, we are going to pay for them in our own body, here on earth, before we die.

Sin carries with it consequences. We will pay for our sins God, has said it will be so. But we go on sinning thinking we are getting away with it, but I am a living witness, that's telling you, that we will give account for everything that we have done. I am living through some consequences that I brought on myself. I endure the suffering now for my own sins, don't let this be you. I have learned that if we obey God, we can save ourselves a lot of pain. This is a warning, so that if you will listen you won't have to go through the pain that I do another scripture that supports this fact is

(Psalms 119:75)
I know, oh lord, that thy judgements are right and that thou in faithfulness hast afflicted me.

From Brokenness to Wholeness

Jeremiah 17:14
Heal me, oh lord and I shall be healed; save me, and I shall be saved: for thou art my praise.

Prayer for Healing

Our father, all wise and everlasting God, our maker, and creator the one that dose all things well. Father, I thank you for all things, please forgive me for all my sins and short comings, help me Lord to lay down all the hurts and disappointments of my past, I know you are able, and I believe that you will. I know it's not your will that we be broken or hurt, so I thank you in advance for your awesome loving care. I thank you for the assurance in knowing that you are faithful to your word. You said that you would never leave us alone or forsake us.

Father, God, please help me. I can't make it without you, I need your help. I am so thankful for all your many wonderful blessings, so thankful that you know me, that you allowed me to know you, you are an awesome God. And Lord, I love you, the best I know how to. I just want to thank you for all things in my life, the good and the bad, because I know you will work them out for my good. It's because of you that I move and have my being, all that I have is because of you. God, I thank you and I come to you Father, because I know you are a healer. You have all power in your hands, and if it be your will, please sir, grant your servant healing, in Jesus' name.

I pray that you will comfort me in my suffering, give skills to the hands of my doctors and bless the

From Brokenness to Wholeness

means used for my healing, give me assurance in the power of your grace, that even when I am afraid, I may still be able to put my trust in you in Jesus's name. heal me Lord, and I shall be healed, save me and I shall be saved, for thou art my praise. Amen.

Epilogue

No one can live a productive life bound by hurt and pain from their past. We have a loving God, that came that we might have life and have it more abundantly. If your life is broken and you are bound by things that have happened in your past, break free as you read this book and walk with the woman at the well and I. We will share with you the tools that Jesus shared with us, to a better life in him. Seeing how Jesus set her free, how he set me free, and if you use the tools given in these pages, you too can be set fee.

The women in this book were broken but no longer held captive by their past, because Jesus meet them at the well. He will make a special trip just for you, wherever there is a need, Jesus, will be there to meet your need. He said he would never leave you, nor forsaken you. He can heal you and make you healthy and whole again, giving you a reason to live a prosperous life. Jesus said it was his meat and drink to do the will of his father, and if we take care of his business then he will take care of ours.

From Brokenness to Wholeness

Dianne Walker

From Brokenness to Wholeness

www.ingramcontent.com/pod-product-compliance
Lightning Source LLC
Chambersburg PA
CBHW052119110526
44592CB00013B/1674